People in My Community/La gente de mi comunidad

Veterinarian/
El veterinario

New Lenox
Public Library District
120 Veterans Parkway
New Lenox, Illinois 60451

JoAnn Early Macken
photographs by/fotografías de Gregg Andersen

Reading consultant/Consultora de lectura: Susan Nations, M.Ed., author/literacy coach/consultant

WEEKLY WR READER
EARLY LEARNING LIBRARY

Please visit our web site at: www.earlyliteracy.cc
For a free color catalog describing Weekly Reader® Early Learning Library's
list of high-quality books, call 1-877-445-5824 (USA) or 1-800-387-3178 (Canada).
Weekly Reader® Early Learning Library's fax: (414) 336-0164.

Library of Congress Cataloging-in-Publication Data available upon request
from publisher. Fax (414) 336-0157 for the attention of the Publishing
Records Department.

ISBN 0-8368-3676-6 (lib. bdg.)
ISBN 0-8368-3690-1 (softcover)

First published in 2003 by
Weekly Reader® Early Learning Library
330 West Olive Street, Suite 100
Milwaukee, WI 53212 USA

3 1984 00218 8728

Art direction: Tammy Gruenewald
Page layout: Katherine A. Goedheer
Photographer: Gregg Andersen
Editorial assistant: Diane Laska-Swanke
Translators: Colleen Coffey and Consuelo Carrillo

Printed in the United States of America

1 2 3 4 5 6 7 8 9 07 06 05 04 03

Note to Educators and Parents

Reading is such an exciting adventure for young children! They are beginning to integrate their oral language skills with written language. To encourage children along the path to early literacy, books must be colorful, engaging, and interesting; they should invite the young reader to explore both the print and the pictures.

People in My Community is a new series designed to help children read about the world around them. In each book young readers will learn interesting facts about some familiar community helpers.

Each book is specially designed to support the young reader in the reading process. The familiar topics are appealing to young children and invite them to read — and re-read — again and again. The full-color photographs and enhanced text further support the student during the reading process.

In addition to serving as wonderful picture books in schools, libraries, homes, and other places where children learn to love reading, these books are specifically intended to be read within an instructional guided reading group. This small group setting allows beginning readers to work with a fluent adult model as they make meaning from the text. After children develop fluency with the text and content, the book can be read independently. Children and adults alike will find these books supportive, engaging, and fun!

Una nota a los educadores y a los padres

¡La lectura es una emocionante aventura para los niños! En esta etapa están comenzando a integrar su manejo del lenguaje oral con el lenguaje escrito. Para fomentar la lectura desde una temprana edad, los libros deben ser vistosos, atractivos e interesantes; deben invitar al joven lector a explorar tanto el texto como las ilustraciones.

La gente de mi comunidad es una nueva serie pensada para ayudar a los niños a conocer el mundo que los rodea. En cada libro, los jóvenes lectores conocerán datos interesantes sobre el trabajo de distintas personas de la comunidad.

Cada libro ha sido especialmente diseñado para facilitar el proceso de lectura. La familiaridad con los temas tratados atrae la atención de los niños y los invita a leer — y releer — una y otra vez. Las fotografías a todo color y el tipo de letra facilitan aún más al estudiante el proceso de lectura.

Además de servir como fantásticos libros ilustrados en la escuela, la biblioteca, el hogar y otros lugares donde los niños aprenden a amar la lectura, estos libros han sido concebidos específicamente para ser leídos en grupos de instrucción guiada. Este contexto de grupos pequeños permite que los niños que se inician en la lectura trabajen con un adulto cuya fluidez les sirve de modelo para comprender el texto. Una vez que se han familiarizado con el texto y el contenido, los niños pueden leer los libros por su cuenta. ¡Tanto niños como adultos encontrarán que estos libros son útiles, entretenidos y divertidos!

— Susan Nations, M.Ed., author, literacy coach,
and consultant in literacy development

A veterinarian is sometimes called a vet. A vet helps keep animals healthy. A vet takes care of animals that are sick or hurt.

— — — — — — — —

Algunas veces el veterinario se llama el "vet". El veterinario ayuda a mantener saludables a los animales. Cuida de los animales que están enfermos o heridos.

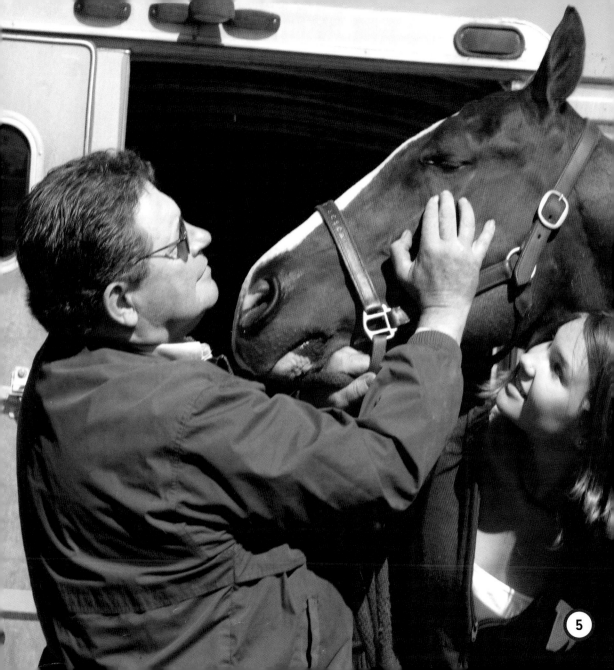

Vets examine animals and give them medicine. They clean teeth, operate, and set broken bones.

- - - - - - - -

Los veterinarios examinan a los animales y les dan medicinas. Les limpian los dientes, los operan y les arreglan los huesos rotos.

Some vets take care of people's pets. They might work in an office or an animal hospital.

━ ━ ━ ━ ━ ━ ━ ━

Algunos veterinarios cuidan a las mascotas de las personas. Pueden trabajar en un consultorio o en un hospital para animales.

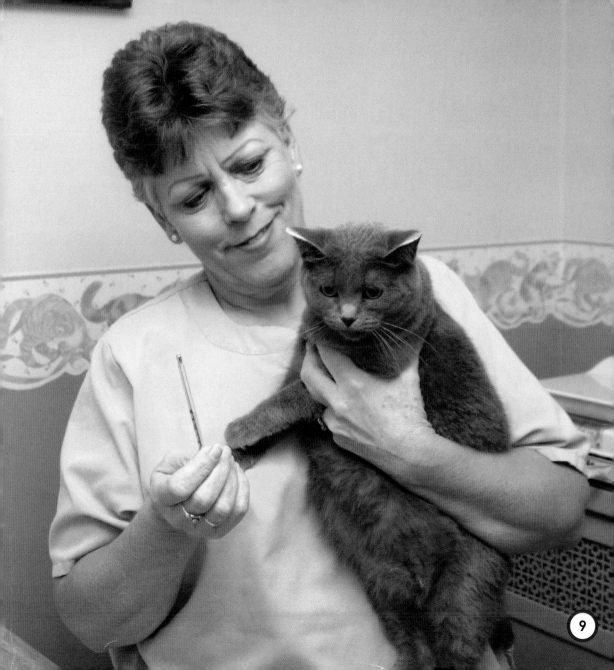

Some vets take care of farm animals. They might visit a farm to treat horses, cows, sheep, or **pigs**.

- - - - - - -

Otros cuidan los animales de las granjas. Ellos pueden visitar las granjas para tratar los caballos, las vacas, las ovejas o los **cerdos**.

pig/cerdo

Some vets take care of animals in a zoo. Others treat wild animals. Wild animals can be dangerous!

Algunos veterinarios cuidan a los animales en el zoológico. Otros tratan animales salvajes. ¡Los animales salvajes pueden ser peligrosos!

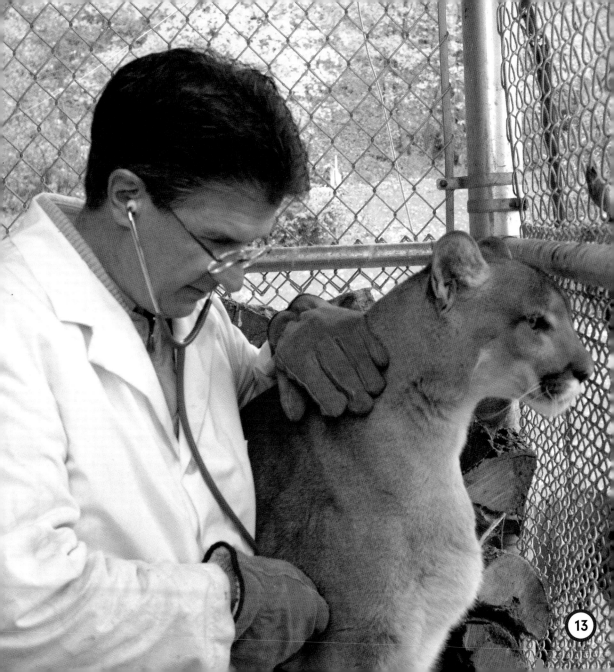

Like doctors for people, vets use tools to help their patients. A vet looks in an animal's eyes, ears, and mouth.

— — — — — — —

Como los médicos para las personas, los veterinarios usan instrumental para ayudar a sus pacientes. Examinan los ojos, los oídos y la boca de los animales.

A vet uses a **stethoscope** to hear an animal's heartbeat and breathing.

— — — — — — —

El veterinario usa un **estetoscopio** para oír los latidos del corazón y la respiración de los animales.

stethoscope/ estetoscopio

17

A vet uses a thermometer to take an animal's temperature. A vet uses **X-rays** to see an animal's organs and **bones**.

‑ ‑ ‑ ‑ ‑ ‑ ‑ ‑

El veterinario usa un termómetro para tomar la temperatura. Usa los **rayos-X** para ver los órganos y los **huesos**.

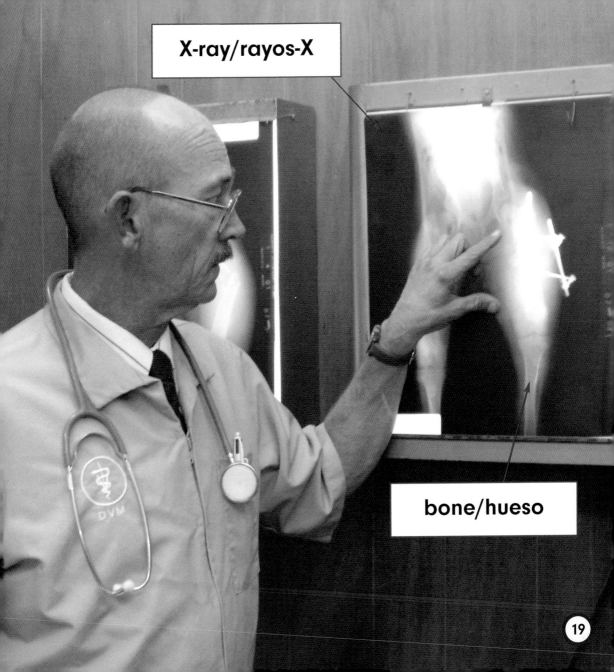

X-ray/rayos-X

bone/hueso

Vets show people how to take good care of animals. If you have a question about your pet, ask a vet.

------- -

Los veterinarios le enseñan a la gente a cuidar bien sus animales. Si tienes algún problema sobre tu mascota, pregunta al veterinario.

Glossary/Glosario

operate – to perform surgery

operar – hacer una cirugía

organs – parts of a body

órganos – partes del cuerpo

temperature – the degree of heat in a body

temperatura – grado de calor del cuerpo

For More Information/Más información

Fiction Books/Libros de ficción

Dodd, Lynley. *Hairy Maclary's Rumpus at the Vet.*
  Milwaukee: Gareth Stevens Publishing, 2000.

Leonard, Marcia. *The Pet Vet.* Brookfield, Conn.: Millbrook
  Press, 1999.

Nonfiction Books/Libros de no ficción

Liebman, Daniel. *I Want to Be a Vet.*
  Toronto: Firefly Books, 2000.

Ready, Dee. *Veterinarians.* Mankato, Minn.:
  Bridgestone Books, 1997.

Web Sites/Páginas Web

**American Veterinary Medical Association's Care
for Animals Kids Corner**
www.avma.org/careforanimals/kidscorner/default.asp
Petpourri animal care activities

Index/Índice

About the Author/Información sobre la autora

JoAnn Early Macken is the author of children's poetry, two rhyming picture books, *Cats on Judy* and *Sing-Along Song* and various other nonfiction series. She teaches children to write poetry and received the Barbara Juster Esbensen 2000 Poetry Teaching Award. JoAnn is a graduate of the MFA in Writing for Children Program at Vermont College. She lives in Wisconsin with her husband and their two sons.

JoAnn Early Macken es autora de poesía para niños. Ha escrito dos libros de rimas con ilustraciones, *Cats on Judy* y *Sing-Along Song* y otras series de libros educativos para niños. Ella enseña a los niños a escribir poesía y ha ganado el Premio Barbara Juster Esbensen en el año 2000. JoAnn se graduó con el título de "MFA" en el programa de escritura infantil de Vermont College. Vive en Wisconsin con su esposo y sus dos hijos.